AI WORLD
AI IN CARS

by Ford Chambers

pogo

Ideas for Parents and Teachers

Pogo Books let children practice reading informational text while introducing them to nonfiction features such as headings, labels, sidebars, maps, and diagrams, as well as a table of contents, glossary, and index.

Carefully leveled text with a strong photo match offers early fluent readers the support they need to succeed.

Before Reading

- "Walk" through the book and point out the various nonfiction features. Ask the student what purpose each feature serves.
- Look at the glossary together. Read and discuss the words.

Read the Book

- Have the child read the book independently.
- Invite them to list questions that arise from reading.

After Reading

- Discuss the child's questions. Talk about how they might find answers to those questions.
- Prompt the child to think more. Ask: Would you like to ride in a self-driving car? Why or why not?

Pogo Books are published by Jump!
5357 Penn Avenue South
Minneapolis, MN 55419
www.jumplibrary.com

Copyright © 2025 Jump!
International copyright reserved in all countries. No part of this book may be reproduced in any form without written permission from the publisher.

Library of Congress Cataloging-in-Publication Data

Names: Chambers, Ford, author.
Title: AI in cars / by Ford Chambers.
Description: Minneapolis, MN: Jump!, Inc., [2025]
Series: AI world | Includes index.
Audience: Ages 7-10
Identifiers: LCCN 2024024889 (print)
LCCN 2024024890 (ebook)
ISBN 9798892135597 (hardcover)
ISBN 9798892135603 (paperback)
ISBN 9798892135610 (ebook)
Subjects: LCSH: Automobiles—Automatic control.
Automobiles—Electronic equipment.
Artificial intelligence.
Classification: LCC TL152.8 .M33 2025 (print)
LCC TL152.8 (ebook)
DDC 629.2220285/63—dc23/eng/20240702
LC record available at https://lccn.loc.gov/2024024889
LC ebook record available at https://lccn.loc.gov/202

Editor: Alyssa Sorenson
Designer: Emma Almgren-Bersie

Photo Credits: Elkins Eye Visuals/Shutterstock, cover; ArtHead/Shutterstock, cover (pattern); JasonDoiy/iStock, 1, 6-7; hxdbzxy/Shutterstock, 3; PonyWang/iStock, 4; Jose Gil/Shutterstock, 5; WendellandCarolyn/iStock, 8; Chesky_W/iStock, 9; Just_Super/iStock, 10-11; AndreyPopov/iStock, 12-13; lv-olga/Shutterstock, 14; ZUMA Press, Inc./Alamy, 15; AlinStock/Shutterstock, 16-17; Prostock-studio/Shutterstock, 18-19; FG Trade/iStock, 20; gremlin/iStock, 20-21; PhonlamaiPhoto/iStock, 23.

Printed in the United States of America at Corporate Graphics in North Mankato, Minnesota.

TABLE OF CONTENTS

CHAPTER 1
What Is AI?...4

CHAPTER 2
The Smart Car...8

CHAPTER 3
Self-Driving Cars..14

ACTIVITIES & TOOLS
Try This!...22
Glossary...23
Index..24
To Learn More...24

CHAPTER 1
WHAT IS AI?

A driver is in a car. She doesn't touch the steering wheel. The car drives on its own.

steering wheel

The car has cameras and **sensors**. These notice things around it. The car slows down on its own. Why? The car ahead is too close. This is **artificial intelligence** (AI) at work. AI helps machines and computers do things humans use knowledge and skills to do.

CHAPTER 1

Vehicles can use AI in many ways. Some AI controls a car for a little while. It **steers** the car to safety. If a person is in the road, AI can tell. It uses the brakes. This stops the car. Some vehicles use AI to drive all by themselves!

CHAPTER 2
THE SMART CAR

AI can avoid crashes. How? It sees road lines. It warns the driver if the car goes out of its lane.

lane

Some parking spots are tricky to fit into. The driver lets AI take over. AI steers the car. It parks the car in the space.

CHAPTER 2

Many cars have cruise control. This controls a car's speed. AI goes a step further. How? It senses vehicles ahead of the car. AI adjusts the car's **pace** to match. A vehicle ahead slams on its brakes. AI slows the car down. It doesn't crash.

DID YOU KNOW?

Human drivers can see a problem and act in 0.5 seconds. AI notices a problem in 0.3 seconds or less!

CHAPTER 2

Many crashes happen because of sleepy drivers. AI can help. How? Some cars have cameras inside. AI can tell if a driver's eyes look tired. It might ask the driver to take a break. It might slow down the car.

DID YOU KNOW?

Some cars have **voice assistants**. The driver gives a command. The assistant listens. It replies. It can start the car. It can turn on hot or cold air. It can give directions.

CHAPTER 2

CHAPTER 3
SELF-DRIVING CARS

A person orders a ride on a **rideshare app**. The car pulls up. No one is inside. Who is driving? AI! Cameras and sensors see all around.

In 2024, self-driving cars were in a few cities. **Robotaxis** picked up passengers. But sometimes they caused trouble. They blocked traffic. They didn't always know how to respond to emergency vehicles on the road.

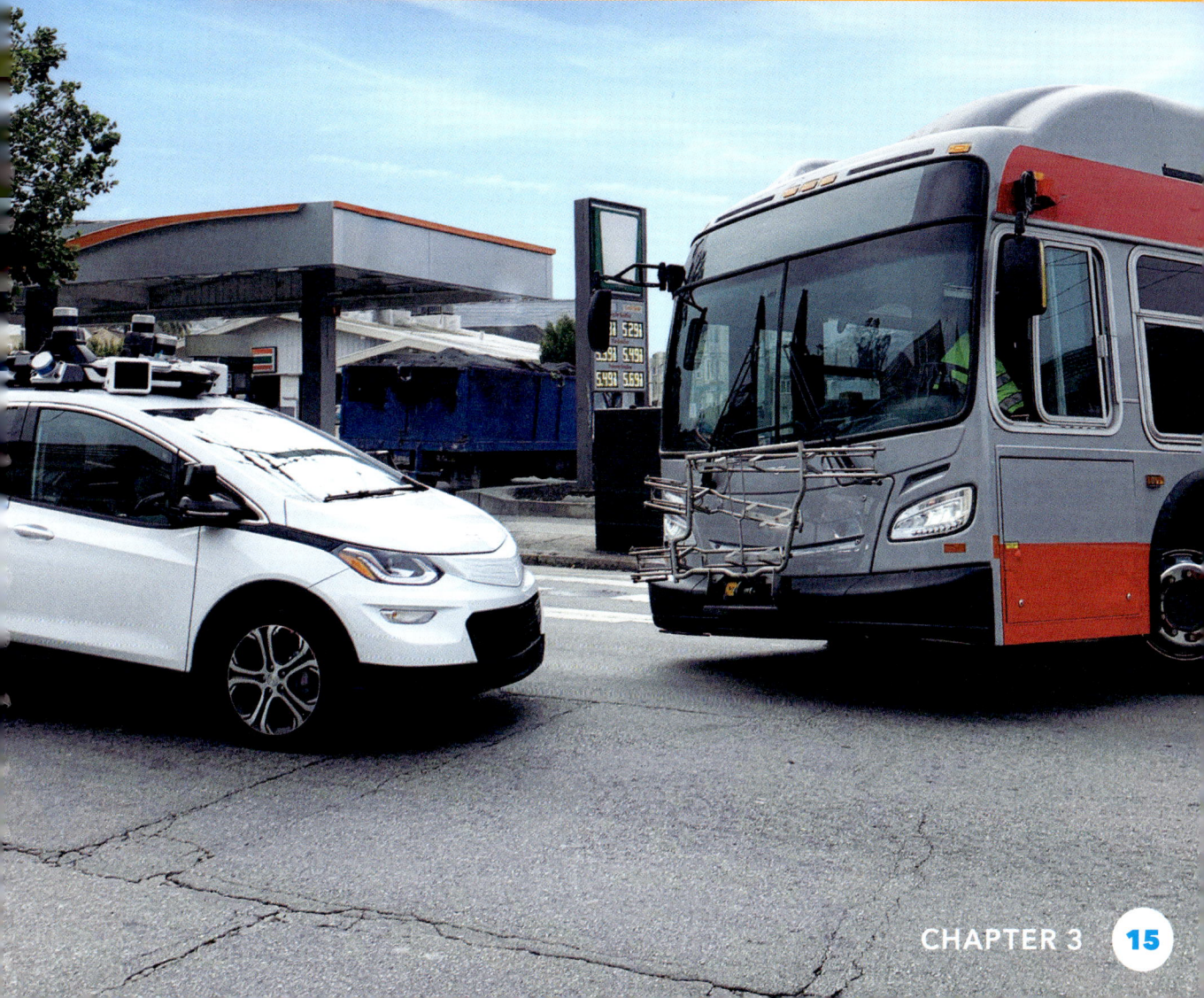

CHAPTER 3   15

Self-driving cars have even gotten into accidents. Many people are working to make AI better. Why? They want all cars to be driverless someday. They believe this will make the roads safer.

16 CHAPTER 3

TAKE A LOOK!

Some cars have more AI control than others. Take a look!

ZERO
A human is in full control.

HIGH
AI drives. No human is needed.

LEVEL OF AI CONTROL →

LOW
AI can do some things. It may brake or steer.

MEDIUM
AI can drive for periods of time, but a driver may need to take over.

In 2024, companies tested fully self-driving vehicles. The cars drove themselves. But a human often had to be at the wheel. Why? AI does not always know what to do. It might have problems in bad weather. Fog and rain can make it hard for sensors to read what is going on. The human driver takes over.

Someday, self-driving vehicles could be everywhere. Self-driving trucks could carry goods. They could drive all day and night. AI doesn't need to sleep. Maybe one day you will have a self-driving car!

DID YOU KNOW?

Cars aren't the only vehicles with AI. Some people are working on self-flying airplanes!

CHAPTER 3

ACTIVITIES & TOOLS

TRY THIS!

CREATE YOUR OWN CAR AI

What else could AI do for cars? Come up with new ideas with this fun activity!

What You Need:
- paper and pencil or a device for taking notes
- a vehicle or a video of a vehicle driving

❶ Go for a ride in a vehicle, or watch a video of someone in a car.

❷ Make a list of what people do in the car. Does AI help? If so, how?

❸ Pick one thing people do in a car that does not use AI. Think about how AI could make that easier or better.

❹ Come up with new AI for driving or cars. How does it work? Does it need sensors or cameras? What decisions does it make? Write down your ideas. Share them with a friend or family member.

GLOSSARY

artificial intelligence: The science of making computers do things that previously needed human intelligence, such as understanding language.

pace: A rate of speed.

rideshare app: An application that sends a message to a ridesharing service.

robotaxis: Taxis driven by AI instead of humans.

sensors: Tools that notice and measure changes.

steers: Makes a vehicle go in a particular direction by moving a wheel.

vehicles: Machines used for carrying people or goods.

voice assistants: AI systems that understand and respond to language.

INDEX

accidents 16
airplanes 20
brakes 6, 10, 17
cameras 5, 13, 14
crashes 8, 10, 13
cruise control 10
lane 8
pace 10
parks 9
passengers 15
rideshare app 14
road lines 8
robotaxis 15
safety 6
self-driving 15, 16, 19, 20
sensors 5, 14, 19
slows 5, 10, 13
steering wheel 4, 19
steers 6, 9, 17
traffic 15
voice assistants 13
weather 19

TO LEARN MORE

Finding more information is as easy as 1, 2, 3.
1. Go to www.factsurfer.com
2. Enter "Alincars" into the search box.
3. Choose your book to see a list of websites.